Ted Pearson grew up on the San Francisco Peninsula. After early musical training, he began writing poetry in 1964. He subsequently attended Vandercook College of Music, Foothill College, and San Francisco State University. In 1976, he published his first book, *The Grit*, and began his ongoing association with the San Francisco Language Poets. Recent books include *Durations* (2022), *Overtures* (2023), and *Early Autumn* (2024). Chamber Music is his thirtieth book of poetry. He lives in Northampton, Massachusetts, with his wife, Sheila Lloyd, and their dog, Kofi.

ALSO BY TED PEARSON

The Grit, 1976, Trike Books (San Francisco)
The Blue Table, 1979, Trike Books (San Francisco)
Soundings, 1980, Singing Horse Press (Philadelphia)
Ellipsis, 1981, Trike Books (San Francisco)
Refractions, 1982, *Origin* (Series 4) (Boston)
Flukes, 1982, Privately Printed (San Francisco)
Coulomb's Law, 1984, Square Zero Editions (San Francisco)
Mnemonics, 1985, Gaz (San Francisco)
Catenary Odes, 1987, O Books (Oakland)
Evidence: 1975–1989, Gaz 1989, (San Francisco)
Planetary Gear, 1991, Roof Books (New York)
Mnèmoniques, 1992, *trans. Françoise de Laroque*, Un bureau sur
                                          l'Atlantique (Royaumont)
Acoustic Masks, 1994, Zasterle Press (Tenerife)
The Devil's Aria, 1999, Meow Press (Buffalo)
Songs Aside: 1992–2002, 2003, Past Tents Press (Detroit)
Encryptions, 2007, Singing Horse Press (San Diego)
Extant Glyphs: 1964–1980, 2014, Singing Horse Press (San Diego)
The Coffin Nail Blues, 2016, Atelos (Berkeley)
After Hours, 2016, Singing Horse Press (San Diego)
An Intermittent Music: 1975–2010, 2016, Chax Press (Victoria, TX)
The Markov Chain, 2017, Shearsman Books (Bristol)
Trace Elements, 2019, Tuumba Press (Berkeley)
Personal Effects, 2019, BlazeVox Books (Kenmore, NY)
Exit Music, 2019, Singing Horse Press (San Diego)
Last Date, 2020, Singing Horse Press (San Diego)
Set Pieces, 2021, Spuyten Duyvil (New York)
Durations, 2022, Selva Oscura Press (Chicago)
Overtures, 2023, BlazeVox Books (Kenmore, NY)
Early Autumn, 2024, Chax Press (Tucson)

Ted Pearson

Chamber Music

Shearsman Books

First published in the United Kingdom in 2024 by
Shearsman Books
PO Box 4239
Swindon
SN3 9FN

Shearsman Books Ltd Registered Office
30–31 St. James Place, Mangotsfield, Bristol BS16 9JB
(this address not for correspondence)

www.shearsman.com

ISBN 978-1-84861-926-5

ACKNOWLEDGEMENTS
Excerpts from 'In the Moment' and 'Interstitial Odes'
were first published in *Creative Flight* (India).

"Music is at once the product of feeling and knowledge."
—Alban Berg

Contents

False Cadences

"I put forward these distinctions as replacements for other distinctions, and against them."
—Jacques Rancière

1.

Between the I that writes and the eye that sees there lies a hellish topography. Death embraces what fear of death denies. In the silence that follows, as death attests, there *is* no paradise.

2.

Life wants a word. By ear, a tune to sing. Then came decades of unrequited labor, when less was never enough. That's when the poet knew to fold lest the Muses call his bluff.

3.

His dreams include the missing and the dead – and a hillside grave where he stands in the rain, his past as near as a childhood fear that lingers like chronic pain.

4.

Every noun has the power to name. Of those in his head, no two are the same. In the empire of darkness, he wants for a flame. Words are his tokens; language his game.

5.

Whose lyrics tell of our present disasters sings from dawn till the cusp of night. Who knows but little knows enough to keep the end of days in sight.

6.

A fate foretold compels who dwells in the gap between now and then. He has no choice but to underwrite a life made real by his pen. And now, with that life in the balance, he's down at the crossroads again.

7.

He lives withal a quiet life in the unquiet wards of the city. He loves his wife – and he loves to write, which he had to learn in stages. Simply to say that he loves her more than he loves his hard-won pages.

8.

Beyond redemption, and thereby damned, wanders the poet by time betrayed. Where heaven is but a blue-sky scam, echoes sound the abyssal depths in which these songs were made.

9.

There was a time when the sting of lust had stymied his advance. That's when he leapt besotted to the waiting arms of chance, only to feel that selfsame sting and once more stand entranced.

10.

Does a still-life grow impatient with time? Do action paintings ever rest? Is an object's status absolute? Is there such a test? A world beyond these walls awaits as sun-drenched streets attest.

11.

In a dream where words are blossoms, he parses roots and stems. And, though his quest might seem absurd, he seeks a Grail made up of words in a world made inconceivable without them.

12.

Who stands on principle falls the farthest, there to take his place. Once he found the words he sought, each an instance of sound as thought, he ordered them with grace.

13.

Sunrise chases off the dreams that plague his endless nights. Then he makes his rounds. His practice abstracts light as song with which the silent dark resounds.

14.

His passion for gratified desire is clear. He's older but lucid as his end grows nearer. Now, he's intent on speaking his mind till his last breath clouds the mirror.

15.

Whenever time is manifest, language comes alive. But something from nothing leaves little we need. We strictly parsed our thoughts and words, but temporized our deeds.

16.

Memory's lapses threaten moments of pleasure. His song's a mnemonic device. Who, having basked in earthly delights, wonders if, absent pleasure itself, remembered pleasure can alone suffice?

17.

When a lifetime of sorrow stilled his speech, language being
out of reach, wordless humming followed. These were the tunes
he learned as a boy without any thought for tomorrow.

18.

The specter of doubt impedes his thinking. His losses beggar
his remaining days. At the sight of his lover fading away, his
readers curse his Orphic gaze.

19.

In the broken figure of the abject suitor we glimpse the re-
mains of a ruined world in love with its ruination. A world
redeemed by grace of existing, despite his bitter ruminations.

20.

Though beauty be mocked, its truth remains. Caught in the
throes of the analytical, poetry parses the language of pain,
which is always already political.

21.

Last words languish in the latticed lines of a strophe left hanging in the balance. Insolvent? Sure. But entire to himself, having burned his bridges behind him.

22.

Contraries constitute the life of the mind. Without them, we're mired in place. Between convictions and maledictions, disjunct scenes compose a world whose scars we can't efface.

23.

Sight and sound form two dimensions of a present in search of depth (as flesh) and time (as life in its passing). The poet battles the anomie within (the modern version of original sin).

24.

Deep in the night of negativity, the brightest star is but a shill. Call it a beacon of paradise lost in a past that never happened for fear of a future that surely will.

25.

A mutinous tongue betrays its secrets, whose faded accent remains intact. Thought evolves as the day advances. Red flags manifest psychic wounds upon a psychic map.

26.

They is one thing. I is another. At the height of its most militant ambition, the violence of language demands a critique. Whence the grammar of these unheard voices that justice bids to speak.

27.

Astrologers say we're incompatible. Such is the problem of other minds. But, in the spirit of full disclosure, what mind *isn't* other, especially to itself?

28.

Mars ascendant, and they live to see it, another spring draws near. From sunrise to sunrise, year to year, they've traveled together countless miles, only to end up here.

29.

His days amount to brilliant moments. His life is the sum of his years. Tucked away in a downtown tower, the poet greets the rising sun, whose light absolves his nightly fears.

30.

Between sexual difference and sexual relations, a gap appears in the history of desire. The subjects in question cleave to their flesh like flames that cleave to their fire.

31.

Assumed identities take their places. A ghostly choir begins to sing. The ghosts are real and have their charms. The poet, too, intends no harm. But he's bad with names and faces.

32.

He writes in praise of bygone days, recalling those once kind enough to share themselves with him. Some, in retrospect, more than others, to whom he was just a whim.

33.

Having stayed the tongues of men and angels, he seeks the language that silence frees. Where matter matters, angels flee, leaving their minions to cop a plea.

34.

Death alone can belay his quest to witness the sublime. His love of fate accepts what is, which yields this paradigm. To see the world each morning, *as if* for one last time.

35.

From finitude, finality. From fortitude, reprieve. Death advances daily. There's little time to grieve. Life being brief, there's work to do before we take our leave.

36.

Nouns are names for other nouns. Verbs beget critiques. Syntax renders the order of things, both common and unique. Antecedents find themselves absorbed by the I that speaks.

37.

Flowers fade faster than the words that describe them. Beauty is more than duration. In spring, they'll return to bloom once again and mirror our aspirations.

38.

Flatliners frolic on flat Earth and dance amid the ruins. Given their cherished facts are lies, nothing is illumined. Are they, then, quite human enough or are they all too human?

39.

Alone together in a crowded room, the poet and his double. Absent faith in a future that deceived them, *hope* is a word they'd no sooner use than ever again believe in.

40.

A choir comprises a conspiracy of tongues which, assembled, become as one. Call it devotion or call it art. Call it a pact with the devil, who owned their souls from the start.

41.

He sees connections wherever he looks. Points of light, in the burgeoning darkness, shine like distant stars. But only the poem – "the *made* poem" – can show them for what they are.

42.

Who dwells among strangers keeps to his rooms. On the frontier's verges, a torture garden blooms. Only now has he come to accept that his exile will end in a foreign tomb.

43.

The dead left countless poems behind. And some continue to haunt the poet, caught in a double bind – between his battles with the current regime and the ravages of time.

44.

It's odd how often the end comes first. As if our lives were afterthoughts, complete with jobs and bosses. With friends and lovers now dispersed, our memories count as losses.

45.

In hell, there's no telling people apart. Good and evil were myths from the start. Mortality earmarked all at birth, except those angels who fell to Earth.

46.

One wrong turn and he landed where they dealt from the bottom of a pack of lies. Now immured in the fictive world, "He wants to say his life is real." Damned if he knows why.

47.

Silence reigns in the gaps between letters with which we form our words. Gaps whereof we cannot speak. We, whose lines, once thought oblique, will prove as true as they are bleak.

48.

True believers spread the grief that follows the terror of true belief. The great dead populate living texts. But, being dead, they know too well exactly what comes next.

49.

"To rise enraptured is to fall in agony." Whence the myth of heaven and hell. Wherever equal opposites attract, extinctions plague the anti-world of the one they found intact.

50.

Absent the strength, if not the desire, to take up the songs of his youth, the poet found yet darker songs with which to speak his truth – darker meaning deeper because closer to his roots.

51.

The restless ocean pounds the shore. Storm waves swell, then break apart, not unlike an aging heart. Wearied by use and past its prime, it beats regardless in common time.

52.

Tourists drift among Arts and Letters. It's date night down at *Café Moderne*. Whose patrons, blind to what they see, are deaf as nails to poetry.

53.

Beyond repair, the ruined city consoles the poet's sense of loss with scenes of terrible beauty. All that remains is beauty's truth, whose telling is his duty.

54.

Circumstance gives no quarter to the poor. The poet and vagrant could be brothers. Whose pains and plaints are all but lost in the merciless silence of others.

55.

Between the eye that seeks and the I that speaks, we've mapped the poet's troughs and peaks. Death affirms what life denies – as on the map that got us here, there *is* no paradise.

In the Moment

"Rhythm must be marked by some sort of sound, but this sound is not itself the rhythm."
—Henry Cowell

1.

Not this is all that. *Not that* is neither.
We, the existent, are wont to roam
beyond where those we conjure speak
of the refuge they call home.

2.

The dead ventriloquize living speech
to insist that at last they're free.
Where lived life fosters the love of fate,
in time it leads to a *fait accompli.*

3.

Nothing exists beyond the field
in which dark matter thrives.
Books once dead now come alive
when their pages grace our eyes.

4.

The calm before the storm belies
the chaos yet to come. Once, we
dreamt of countless days. Now,
contingencies dictate their sum.

5.

Rolling thunder gives voice to lightning.
Lightning illumines these unbound pages.
Each strike chastens the kingdom of night
whose terrors have plagued us for ages.

6.

Sublime extremities of scale define us.
The less said the better, though the least
said it best: we are but specks of cosmic dust
where finite thoughts are laid to rest.

7.

Our labor done, it was as it seemed.
Psychic levers pulled our strings.
Poems gave voice to our extremes,
bearing witness to impossible things.

8.

Is knowledge of death an impediment
to thought or a spur to further thinking?
The winds of discourse power our fate,
which we must face unblinking.

9.

Ever fraught, the history of thought
resembles a *mise en abyme* –
where each according to its nature mirrors
each according to its dreams.

10.

The clouds take on their myriad forms,
shaped by winds and densities,
from which the singer draws her breath,
whose sorrow spans immensities.

11.

The poem, at one with its own devices,
does what it says in each of its guises.
The Fates impassively tip the scales,
the better to dole out our travails.

12.

Desire rides roughshod over our days
in a world of difference and constant change.
As the hands that cast it tempered the gong,
lyrics live on in the voice of the song.

13.

Much like the saint who famously prayed
to be saved, "but not just yet" –
so, too, the poet tried to persuade
his local dive to forgive his debt.

14.

Time configures love's asymmetries.
Lodged in The Golden Book of Affinities,
mated pairs occupy chapters and verses
with lovers' sighs and lovers' curses.

15.

Have you ever wondered (the lyric began)
if to live by your word is to live second hand?
Begging to differ, the last poet sings
of art as a breach in the order of things.

16.

The eternal tomboy taunts you.
"Is that all you've got left?"
Looking for an edge, no doubt,
then leaving you bereft.

17.

The voice in the mirror is not
one's own. Neither is the face.
Who will answer for us when
we're gone without a trace?

18.

It's true. This poem won't write itself,
even as fresh words come to mind,
only to end up printed and bound, there
to languish till the end of time.

19.

Deception's doors are open for viewing.
Flaws in perception beget our undoing.
Thus forewarned, we reason away the fear
that our quest may have led us astray.

20.

Childhood's tales are to no avail
to explain the ravages of age.
Lives lived well, if beyond the pale,
can't be summed in a single page.

21.

Simplicity founds its complex structures
on bedrock immune to seismic ruptures.
Once, these wastelands were our gardens,
tended by those who lived on the margins.

22.

The forecast calls for further hauntings
which pose a menace to the tourist trade.
In fact, those ghosts are the only proof
that of their words our songs are made.

23.

The poet (shown in actual size)
expressed no wish to be saved.
It wasn't the fires of hell he feared,
but the airless dark of the grave.

24.

We came here seeking what can't be found.
That's what makes this sacred ground.
It became a legend, how long we persisted
in our belief that the found existed.

25.

Here is precisely where *there* was possible.
Thus the riddle that stumped the Magus.
We live in the thick of yesterday's future.
Killing time here only serves to age us.

26.

The voices have gone, much like they came,
faceless and nameless and no two the same.
And, though their lyrics were less than ideal,
they led nonetheless to the cusp of the Real.

Series Decay

The principal function of form is to advance our understanding.
—Arnold Schoenberg

1.

Theirs is a tale of breakups and breakdowns, of time-bound elements doomed to inconclusion.

Premature premises captioned their context: an intimate meeting at degree zero.

False doctrines fled from reason's embrace. Hypnagogic jottings spelled the end of days.

Genetic markers outlined libidos. Our latent urges doubled down on this week's whatnots.

Myth-makers catered to frontier fantasies. Each version proved to be one and the same.

2.

Science will attest to the cause of death, but not to the omens we chose to live by.

Death, be it said, is a habit with us. Signs and wonders guide our steps. A Hunter's Moon lights the way.

In the name of reason (an explanatory fiction), just how brisk is the traffic in ephemera?

Agency acts on subconscious urges to stay the palsied hand of Fate.

When self-interest clouds your ethical judgment, crises of conscience are crises of state.

3.

Which is the work of the writer – the act of writing or the written text?

Whereas, the capacity to withhold judgment is the rarest of critical virtues,

a change of genre is a change of mind. The body electric is a social fact that once was science fiction.

We admired the picture in the picture window, framed by caseloads of books.

Many were called, but none replied. Who, then, listens to poetry?

4.

We are seeking the poem at the end of time, a time predicted when the world was young

as the time when words could at last be words, and poems at last be poems.

It is to that end any lyric aspires – not the music, but the silence that defines it and gives it shape and sense.

Then the music, till the two are one and the one sings songs of consequence.

And, though the music will last but a moment, it seems that moment is about to commence.

5.

A poem may be a maze of thoughts, if only thoughts of freedom. In the end, it's a question of what comes next.

The desire that induced it and conditions that produced it persist as traces that underwrite the text.

As a matter of course (the poem would insist), the traces are proof that the poem exists.

One-hit wonders cite inspiration. A lifetime of poems requires concentration.

Do texts begin with the desire to write or the writing that makes our desire legible?

6.

Time lines make the best bios, based as they are on discoverable facts. As if we could know

what anyone thought in the confines of their mind. Assumptions that you can't support result in flying blind.

Where thought is graceful at glacial speeds, indolent artists take their ease.

When soulless plutocrats rule the roost, the stats for suicides get a boost at hash-tag end-of-days.

As the beat goes on, it's dealer's choice. First-class drummers don't keep time, but rather give it voice.

7.

Anomie proved to be a formative experience. The
bosses assumed they were destined

for greatness. Albeit lacking a living wage, the
workers seemed content –

a lie the owners told themselves while they collected
the workers' rent.

For the poor, it sufficed that the air was free. They
had no hope of equity.

Failing death or redistribution, begging remained a
beggar's solution.

8.

From *homo economicus* to *homo in debitum* in just
two generations. As the sun cozies up

to Earth's parched surface, geologic time is itself fore-
shortened. Survivalists lobby for the law

of the jungle, albeit it's now a desert. Tooth and claw
was their prime directive; making do their strength.

You can't turn pages with frostbitten fingers. But
even if books are as kindling to minions,

the fires of knowledge will sweep them before it, and
with them what's left of their leaders.

9.

Tactical thinking won't solve this conundrum. When-
ever objects are subject to scrutiny,

subjects object to the gaze. Thus, we played our
longings by ear. The tides of change

have brought us here, where identity is a fantasy, but
never an object of affection.

That's a privilege reserved for subjects who spared us
from rejection.

Subjects whose mercies hold us in thrall and provide
object lessons to each and to all.

10.

Survivors fear what lies ahead. Unknown numbers
are missing or dead.

We endured the war and several plagues. And the
unsubtle signs of the end of days.

But in fact it's what you don't see coming. The lump.
The bruise. The raspy throat.

The trip-and-fall. The failing eyes. Cheap shots taken
at random by Fate that could only hasten our demise.

It's nothing personal. Read the script. Fate was bored
is our surmise.

11.

I don't remember much these days, but I know that a person's not a number.

Large numbers never marched on the Capitol, but large numbers of *people* did –

people who insisted that their prepositions should find equality under the law.

But historical moments are baited traps. They rely on appeasement to stymie change.

It's our knowledge of facts underlying those traps that warrants our disdain.

12.

The scaffolding collapsed on the gallery floor where we waited to enter our dotage.

Structural failure and overdevelopment lead to a changing skyline.

Global warming and drought account for widespread famine and death.

Wars will be fought over food and water, arable land, and liveable spaces.

Meanwhile, we're on-boarding office bots to train them to take our places.

13.

Advantage bots (in case you wondered). They never die and they don't pay taxes.

Machine language says they simply stop – which is all that mortality amounts to.

Scribes recorded prophecies, which they then burned to the multitude's glee.

Realism touts molecular damage while axioms pass like parrots on their way to a spelling bee.

The future is here, so take a chance. Have you never asked a bot to dance?

14.

The sophist threw junk using every seam. It was his only edge. Exposed as the boy in the bubble. Resolved

as the suicide out on a ledge. Objects are typically indifferent to words, except the words for objects.

My favorite ikon? Christ on a crutch. Too busy preaching to heal himself. Footsore as any tramp.

Meanwhile, there might be an upset in the making. The game remains scoreless in the final frame.

When bubble boy cheered the sophist on, the suicide had to go along. It *was* a great day for a game.

15.

Blind as a fossil, the ancient bard has summoned images from behind dead eyes.

Which is one way of saying, *it is written*. And one way of showing

what was wrought. A nude in the likeness of a virile youth has shocked the unsuspecting,

on whose behalf the docent affirms that it's strictly a period piece.

In a later version, the youth has wings. And the bard, in his cups, is about to sing.

16.

In the beginning, when all was Void, there were endless options to be deployed.

Creation myths are those that leave us to repair the damage that they've done.

And of all the "creatives" competing here, this is the sophistry that won.

The handsome nude in the foyer will succeed in engaging viewers as time goes by –

its taut skin flowing from brush to canvas through the gleam in the painter's eye.

17.

    The concept of peaceful coexistence predates our
entry into history. Perhaps

    to return when the inland sea's a swamp and all the
forests barren –

    as if mass extinction were a phase to be gone through
and not the end of our species.

    This time no one walks away. Our love of slaughter
keeps us in the lists.

    The grand experiment is almost over. We cannot
coexist.

18.

    Wherever ethics are pushed aside, ambition isn't a
good look. In the poet's words, "People are starving."

    We want justice, and we want it now. And if that
doesn't rouse you from sleep,

    I'm not sure anything will. Otherwise, it's an ordinary
day. As the sun struggles

    to burn through the fog, skeptical speech says "It
won't make it." But watching serves to pass the time.

    And now another crisis has landed on your porch –
same-day delivery by an Amazon in her prime.

19.

Auspices point to possible futures. Consequences lag behind pyramid schemes.

When language fails to win the day, striking workers pack their tools and slowly walk away.

Why do ghosts get to live rent free? Or the dead who dwell in posterity? Me? I'm stuck with

a worried mind. Once, while parsing a double bind, my screen was filled by a madman's screed.

Which would have been even more disturbing had it been addressed to me.

20.

Halcyon days in the torture garden quietly pass in review. "Much wrong.

A little rightness." That was how the old man put it, evincing a glimpse of what

might have been, which is everything that never was and now may never be.

Of course, we wanted the best for you. And now that it's yours, we're relieved.

At least you know what's been given to you, if not what you have received.

Trance Music

"Where the eye divides, the ear connects."
—John Luther Adams

1.

In 1937, John Cage proposed that we replace the concept of *music* with *the organization of sound*. This applies to poetry as well. Phonemes sound the triad we use to summon the voice of the poem.

2.

Discrepant lyrics assume you're in pain on the grounds that to live is to suffer. Hence, they choose to concern themselves with what you *know* of your feelings. Not as a matter of sympathy, but to stop your mind from reeling.

3.

In 1937, Cage also predicted the birth of electronic music. One result would be a large, if mathematically precise palette – one whose modes would reflect our moods as we moved through the weathers of the world.

4.

A gap exists between the poet and her readers. She's always been her first reader, her toughest critic, and her own most generous interpreter. But hopefully not her last. Because by the time you read her poem, she will have since moved on.

5.

Habits typically include the limitations imposed by their mechanics. There's *what* we read and *how* we read, and differences abound. Hence new readings emerge over time until they, too, become old habits. And the poem begins anew.

6.

There's an intimate pact between the singer and her song, a melding of sound and sense. And all that each expects of the other is all they have to give – even as they've already given whatever there was to give.

7.

Tell us, they said, on whose authority is this *percussion* music? Let's just call it the principle of form. Note the rhythmic patterns of the keystrokes, the variations in tempo and timbre, and quotes from the classic rudiments. Now tell *us* on whose behalf is this *not* percussion music?

8.

The mythographers say that, late in the war, after the vanguard was carried off, outliers carried the day. Of course, they knew what we didn't, which is what made their visions real. That, in the end, was for us to find out and their poems as such to reveal.

9.

When they ask what kind of poems I write, I say the kind with words. Of course, there are also silences to deal with. And between them echoes from the distant past. These resemble memories that you weren't sure would last.

10.

Your heart *beats* and your nerves *hum*, which, assuming you live on Earth, is as quiet as it gets. The low-ghost authors what you think to say, and the tourists call it inspiration. But that train's long since left the station while one word waited for another.

11.

Sound and sense are born of silence. And it's never a *choice* to abandon song. Some there are who were born to sing while others speak their piece. When language does what it does best, sound and sense become as one till silence begs surcease.

12.

The lover of phonemes seeks to find where speech and Eros intertwine with form to structure the embodied mind. Opposed to closure though we are, there's a natural end to each of these rimes. That occurs when the gamut is run an unspecified number of times.

13.

Playing the changes felt like playing in chains, a slave to the music of which one had dreamed. The elders thought we lacked restraint in our search for a love supreme. The end of their era was bound to come, much like the logic of a dream.

14.

Who could improve on Bird's stunning essays or Bud's command of the keys? Commerce said to slow things down and funkify the harmonies. Staying on the cutting edge had rarely paid the rent. And steady work doing what you love was tougher to get than we dreamt.

15.

The rise of rock confounded the elders. It blew right past established markets, even as it helped to define and exploit the nascent world of teens. Hence, except for the fortunate few, it was play with a back beat or keep living lean. And that's when the choir, to which we preach, reminded us "lean is clean."

16.

Schoenberg was asked to explain his method. "It's none of your business," he said. Who also said the eraser is as vital as the lead. He knew the crowd for classics would keep him in arrears. With plenty of chestnuts to go around, tonality, which ruled the roost, was loath to disappear.

17.

The new music sparked a sonic revolution divisive of more than generations. When everything you know is called into question, you can learn to listen or take a stand and try to answer as best you can. Then, of a sudden, your dreams resound with sounds like music makes.

18.

Nobody said it would be easy. The way like letters cling to like makes the lexicon look like a lunch room. Not a good look, but you take what you've been given – including words loath to appear in a poem. To which it is said "no one listens."

19.

When logarithms displaced intuitions, the poet's blood ran cold. It's often said, shit happens, but that saw's getting old. We're better off without myths and deities. And, if our words have tweaked the future, they did so only as anomalies in the unpublished annals of time.

20.

Why do statements regarding art so rarely show their regard? Surrounded by shadows and ambient sounds, the audience soon grew restive. They wanted candlelight and strings to sway to, just like marionettes. They wanted it to be like it used to be – or as close as they could get.

21.

Theater embodies the art of persuasion. If we're done here, let's have drinks. Transitions are based on what you will, while poems say only what they think. In a letter, the aging Williams wrote, "There is nothing more to say." And, in saying precisely that, poetry was there that day.

22.

Who would make of the poem a coherence must account for any disorder at its borders. Daily practice is a constant in a life made possible by friends. Otherwise autonomous, his story ends with nothing left to suture. His creditors have sold his past to fund their stake in his future.

23.

Lies were told of solitary pleasures to demean my imaginary friend. And, although he *is* a ghost, his loyalty knows no end. Being dead, he's long since learned to sing his kind to sleep. Later, we'll meet up back at the club and begin our midnight creep.

24.

The cosmos was still a bit raw at the edges, right where expansion chafed the most. While those who remained at the heart of things were stealthy as veteran ghosts. A late-night dream and a cup of Joe was how it all began. And now the revolution's done and the cosmos continues to expand.

25.

When nothing stays where it belongs, something's bound to give. Being, we say, is an end to becoming, but what has *doing* done? Our best? Who knows? But we've done no better. There's nothing to defend. Especially now, as we reach our end, which is why you don't see us in your future.

26.

The Magus said to say nothing of your practice. To keep things to yourself. First, there's the danger you'll be understood. Second, there's bound to be some prevarication because, third, you don't have a clue. When you read what they say you've written, the author's a stranger to you.

27.

Absurdity obviates the least of our actions, which pleases you no end. Given time, the impossible outlasts you. Why, then, begin what is certain to fail, be it hunting snarks or chasing Grails. Not that we expected the species to last. But, its demise, though certain, waits, while ours is closing fast.

28.

It isn't death but dying he fears, though death is lodged in his every desire, if not in desire itself. Between what's clear and what's opaque, once you consider what's at stake, our needs precede what we think we want, though one is as transient as the other.

29.

The poet escorted himself into exile, about as alone as he gets. Whose victories came without acclaim felt every defeat in his depths. It was there that he sought his defining moment, free of pain, if short of breath. Where to live is to keep absolutes at bay, the last absolute is death.

30.

As fugitive thoughts are to savvy readers, fugitive sounds are to thoughtful ears. Say that these songs *were* composed. How does that matter to you? Test your limits with your native tongue. Not only for what it says it does, but for what, being said, it can do.

Interstitial Odes

"Music, in performance, is a type of sculpture."
—Frank Zappa

1.

It is not "the despair
    of poetry" that "there's
        nothing more to say."

    Rather, it's when there's
        nothing to say that
            poetry is renewed.

        Given the Void from
            which all things flow –
                first came language,

    then lyrics; first came
        melody, then song –
            which we've been

saying all along – years
    we wouldn't care to
        remember, unless, if we

    could have them back, death
    could be forestalled.
        Otherwise, what's

        the point in mourning
            the loss of pleasures
                beyond recall.

2.

To begin in despair is
       to be preferred to ending
              there one day. Thus,

      we began with little
           hope that now we're
               here they'll let us

        stay. Having searched
            our distant past, they say
                we're dinosaurs – by

     which they mean old
        and in the way. As if
           there were somewhere

they needed to be, no matter
      how short of paradise. In
         fact, we left those precincts

     off the map, which
        took them down a peg.
          Now, we're vagrants

       on our hometown streets,
           but we're still too proud
         to beg.

3.

About that angel, a vigorous
        construct, it's an agent of
                wrath and retribution.

      Strictly old testament,
            enraged by a world
                  that has failed to

         find its way. It seems
            the angel has seen
                many worlds, but
  few as hopeless as this
      one. A single day of
          shopping was more

than he could stand.
    As though only poetry
        could stay his hand,

    he scoured the shelves
        but found there none.
           So which fell short,

      the poet or angel? And
        which knows better
           the failure to come?

4.

The arc of his exploits came
        and went. He was left with
                "an intensity of being."

        Inertial guidance plotted
                his course, though he had
                        his moments of discernment.

                To search without stopping or
                        ever finding was not the obsession
                                it first appeared.

        But all that talk of paradise
                had left its mark on his
                        early years. "Would there

be all this searching
        if the found existed?"
                A modest proposal he

        could never resist. Abjuring
                vengeance was easy enough,
                        but his mandate

                (so the poet thought)
                        was to guard future seekers
                                against the sought.

5.

The angel approached
    the temple of love, led there
        by Fate and a godless poet.

    Even the mad have their
        lucid moments. "The stain
            of love

        is upon the world."
            The love of slaughter
                most of all. This

    constitutes a mistranslation
        from the gospel straight to
            the living blues. Not for

nothing has he paid his dues. Yet,
    despite his famed clairvoyance,
        the poet's mood

    was rarely buoyant.
        Nor do our sorties show
            progress from the air.

        Whence calls the Grail,
            from across the abyss, to abandon
                both hope *and* despair.

6.

Having passed the point
        of no return, it's time
                that we pressed on. Our

        passion may be sated, but
                our quest resumes at dawn.
                        To create a book

                that explains the world is
                        surely a mad projection.
                                But to live a bare life

        in hope of heaven
                is to dwell in self-deception.
                        Which presumes a self

exists, if only to be
        deceived. But where are we
                to find such a one

        that isn't already bound to
                its illusions? That isn't already
                        in love with itself?

                One, whose enabling fictions
                        have yet to secure its place
                                in the world.

7.

Peace on Earth is an
    oxymoron. Nice idea,
        wrong planet. A distinctly

   human failing. The
    angel has tipped
        his arrows with

    sorrow. Our fondest
      joys were lost on
        the wing. It was always

  in his nature to make
    those arrows sting.
      Meanwhile, adept

at playing the Fool,
    defeated by language,
      excluded by rule –

  the last Romantic
    died at odds with
      the exploits of his

    youth. Which, when he came
      to define his era, was one more
        bitter truth.

8.

The omniscient narrator
  has been debunked. So
    what were they doing

  at the beach? Free agents
    roam through a free country,
      sans particulars

    of time or place, save
      they are "at the beach."
        Assume there's a sun

  that burns through the fog,
    and therefore assume
      that it's morning.

Assume as well that we're still
  in mourning for a country
    not yet free. You can't

  forget what you've never
    seen, but rest assured,
      it's not a dream.

    A vision, then, in
      which dead tyrants
        burn like effigies.

9.

Life on the outside
        is spent looking in.
                To see what they've

        done still gets under
                your skin. The loss
                        of time accelerates

                with age. Absent
                        friends crowd an
                                empty stage. Those

        in the know say the
                show must go on.
                        Without you, of course,

and without your songs.
        Nor does it matter
                that the score is blank.

        They have only themselves
                to thank. And silence is sure
                        to thin their ranks.

                Meanwhile, the sun-god danced
                        about. Reciting his mantra,
                                "When in doubt, go out."

10.

Eternity brackets our mortal
    remains for the time we are
        given to live. Time to grieve

   the end of time and all those
      true believers. The poet says
         his work will last as long as

     there are readers. Not
        that it matters to
           the Great Extinction.

   But long enough
     to bring him to the
        outskirts of distinction.

He returned to witness
   the end of his tribe.
     Whence comes the poem

   at the end of the mind –
     the final fruit, the bitter
        rind – which coincides

   with the end of time,
     time enough for
        one last rhyme.

Bedtime Tales

"The transition from the neuronal to the mental supposes negation and resistance."
—Catherine Malabou

1.

There's no easy way to say this.

In time, we'll all be dead.

How many facts to prove a point?

How many buttons on your blazer?

Once thought is shown to be finite,

will all further thought be idle?

2.

If turnabout is fair play, why

not disburse your ill-gotten

gains? What would it take

to make reparations? Try

to keep your answers brief

so we know when you start lying.

3.

How very seductive to think of
    "a peace that surpasses understanding."
        That's the kind of assurance one needs
    before heading off to slaughter. I think
        of the old men who sent us there
        and said to give no quarter.

4.

To what end do we contemplate
    the problem of other minds?
        It feels like waking from someone
    else's dream or humming a tune
        you've never heard. Your heart begins
        to lighten, and you feel a bit absurd.

5.

What about these sleights of mind,
      and what about your readers? Hanging
           by one hand from the Tower of Babel,
      and holding your book in the other.
           Have they grown so desperate that
                 they'll trust a book by its cover?

6.

I can barely recognize the person said
      to have written the works I've written.
           Not that I want to distance myself
      from all the work he's wrought. Only
           that it seems like a lifetime ago since
                 we finished each other's thoughts.

7.

About the Grail, there's little to say.
     It appeared one morning and was gone
         in a day. A typical day in a poet's life.
     The online word-of-the-day was *strife*.
         Call its appearance an ontic test, to see
            if the poet would take up the quest.

8.

After years of sleeping rough,
     the poet needed rest. Midway through
         the sleep he craved, he woke and felt
     depressed. His failure to find
         that bloody Grail has left him
            homeless, friendless, and obsessed.

9.

The story as such is endless,
        but stories always end. That's
                when readers catch their breath.
        The quest in question will also end,
                if not in finding the missing Grail,
                        then with the poet's death.

10.

Once, he strolled the boulevards
        and gave no thought to the morrow.
                It seemed enough just to be alive.
        Now, he wanders a barren waste,
                left to wonder if the Grail itself was
                        ever anything more than a lie.

11.

The crowd was local. This, their dive.
        The dialect spoken was larded with jive.
                It seemed we were in an earlier era, but
the music? That was something to hear.
                Changes flew by and made it clear. Folks
                        came to listen and brought their ears.

12.

The tenor preached to the converts,
        a mix of joy and pain. The drums
                were as crisp as the tip of a whip
while the bassist walked the refrain.
        Then, the piano, soft and low,
                showed us another way to go.

13.

Desire gave way to consumption,
    which swayed between want and need.
        Consumers had myriad sources
    to satisfy their greed. Then,
        one day, the consumers themselves
        became commodities.

14.

Who keeps the keys,
    locks the locks. Surveillance
        runs around the clock.
    But once your ship has
        left the dock, the city
           gates swing wide.

15.

That was then. This is how.

    They took the image for the thing

        itself and played their games of chance.

    The mind sees what it wants to see.

        But, try as they might, they still can't tell

            the dancer from the dance.

16.

They can no longer tell

    their needs from desires.

        The latter are dreams

    to which they aspire,

        while their needs insist

            their condition is dire.

17.

Is choice a matter of want
      or will? Which takes
            precedence? Which defers?
      First, factor in what you
          know of desire, and
               then what you'd prefer.

18.

Poetry has little to say for
      itself, but does acknowledge
          that sound and sense are
      equal sources of meaning.
          And it posits *that* we write
             in lieu of lucid dreaming.

19.

Early autumn. I remember April.
  The woman's name was April
    and our time together charmed.
  Forensics ransacked hearth and home.
    There were no sentient beings harmed
      in the making of this poem.

20.

She said to dial it up a notch.
  "Your portfolio isn't glamorous."
    Hard truth always whets my
taste for whisky and for cannabis.
    Some critiques are hard to take.
      I thought that she said "amorous."

21.

When government devolved
     into a partisan shit-storm,
          staffers sold umbrellas.
     Then they grew the GDP
          with their aggrandized
          bestsellers.

22.

Abstractions flirt with fresh conceits.
     Active verbs go against the beat.
          Perhaps it's time to bring back the sonnet.
     You could write a new series
          on the history of thought
          and put some English on it.

23.

Fresh blood's needed to replenish
    the vanguard. Death has blunted
        the tip of the spear, but that
    won't relieve the precarity of those
        death chose to leave behind. That's
            now *your* job to bear in mind.

24.

On reaching an evolutionary
    impasse, the species agreed to
        diverge. Thus did a gambit
    to survive become a grab for power.
        Political animals have their quirks.
            Regime maps update on the hour.

25.

Mythopœia was coined in the Thirties.
            Generations of fan boys followed.
                  Terabytes were post-avant.
            Virtual reality sought detente.
                  It falls to us to clean up the mess
                        when truth exposes myth's excess.

26.

Grand illusions disturb my work.
            I include them when I can.
                  Not that anything need be explained.
            Where affect wavers, attention roams.
                  Now, observe as another illusion
                        approaches to enter the poem.

27.

When the blue hour yields to
    The World of Blues, we turn off
        the evening news. Judgment is partial
    to its known effects. Copyists introduced
        corruptions in the text. Rhythmic cues
      led to what came next.

28.

Why write – and I've asked this before –
    unless one has "the flaw *par excellence,*
        the appetite to exist?" That, and words,
    without which, there's nothing to be said.
      Poetry, though unforgiving,
        gives us life, if not a living.

www.ingramcontent.com/pod-product-compliance
Lightning Source LLC
Chambersburg PA
CBHW022202080426
42734CB00006B/539